Kingdom

poems

Michael Cadnum

Horse Eagle Press,
Albany, California

2

3

Acknowledgments

These poems have appeared in the following publications:

America

> Crocodile, Magpie Harm

Blue Unicorn

> Hibernation, The Louse

Commonweal Magazine

> Ants, The Bee, Bee Swarm, Cat, Jack Rabbit, Eagle, Egret, The Elephant at the Mall Grand Opening, The Giraffe, Flea, Mosquito, The Moth, Opossum, Otter, The Roe Deer, Racoon, Sandpiper, Termite Damage, Vulture, Wasps, Whales

Poem

> Turtles

4

For Sherina

Red kayak, blue paddle, morning star

5

Table of Contents

6

Foreword

Michael Cadnum's *Kingdom*

Anyone who really wants to *see* the world will read and reread these animal poems: *Kingdom.*

Cadnum sometimes likes speaking for an animal that doesn't seem to have much to be said for it. Or he celebrates them—enters into their point of view. He goes far, not just opossum, a clumsy, hapless creature, but also the louse, the flea, the termite. In the other direction, magnificent or beautiful animals: the whale, the eagle, the otter. Difference is the point.

Beyond speaking for the animals, however, the poems do something big. They set up the Ecological World, the world other than us. The world we're ruining because we don't see it, even when we are looking at it. We don't see the power of the otherness.

The order of the poems sets this up. The animals appear in reverse alphabetical order: Whales to Ants. To reverse the alphabet is to reverse the human priority.

With humans backed off a little, we might see otherness. The Kingdom is wildly myriad. Some animals have to be seen to be believed. Some, the better seen, the harder to believe. Cadnum makes us—teaches us—to see them. We see they are utterly different, and perfectly coherent. Worlds, in fact.

Some are cosmic. Whales link to stars. Turtles to fire. The moth is "on his way with earth towards morning." Light is the lizard's body. Otter is a tide and is "uttered" by the ocean. Eagle--very powerful--"releases the earth/every dawn." At the end, we see that beneath the ant "crawls the world."

Some poems are myths of origin: Whales and turtles. The opossum is "Surely a first creature/early in Creation's chapters." Paradoxically, the better the animals are seen, the more they are transformed. Which means seeing is transforming—the seeing that is art and poetry.

But animals will always be emblems and metaphors of the human. You'll recognize them. Some animals, seen in what humans call evolution, are doing what the animals call learning. This is a neat reversal. "And so we learned," say the turtles. "We muscled over our frailty/a new comprehension."

This may sound abstract, but first and last, every poem is a pleasure to read. "How will he do it this time?" you ask as he starts a poem like Scorpion. He does.

Rosemary Deen,
Poetry Editor
Commonweal Magazine

9

Whales

The whales got too big and had to go back into the water.

A mother to her child, overheard at a museum

Even when we no longer ran,
for years, the hills
comforted, the pine-wood
brushed our broad, bony paws.
Sun kneaded the hair along
our spine, and rain
combed it warm and
easy under the dawn.
Each taste of living food,

quick and hot, was strength
and daylight was a giant room.
Bird shadow whispered across our eyelids
and slow voles flattened
under the browse

of our jowls. It could not
bear, the grass, the rain-brushed
soil. Night was threadbare,

wearing thin, wearing through.
One more afternoon, we prayed,
one more sunrise.
Gravel parted hard
beneath our plowing
preludes, voice to voice.
And when the weariness began
we could not name it, we

who had coursed over
the hill, plunged valley,
tossed free in the cold
morning light. Years since we had
danced, we thought: we are dancers.
Until we could not pretend, until the stone

sky pressed, and each breath hauled a
quarry in, and pushed it out again,
each heartbeat the grinding of ore
on ore. Such rooted
exhaustion we could not lift
a song. Nosing the tang of foam-spume,

shivering, chest to surf.
We were tongues. We were wet
as eyes. No one would know
us, we would have no name.
Without a star we drank
the black salt. And began.

Wasps

Ripe plums and the hibiscus
are their swag and nothing
can withstand their slash and wheel.
Like the machine gun and the spiteful neighbor
they repeat and repeat again--
no fist or curse can quell them.
They spend their winters in the earth
and hibernate during the sifting storms,
and what they dream
and what faith moves them
as they awaken I just begin to guess.
There is no legend of this amber shrapnel,

no myth of their beginning.
The late winter days weaken, settling cool
and harmless over the fields.
And then one afternoon
this legion captures the sunlight,
fencing with the hummingbirds they can
kill with a single touch, securing the honeysuckle

without will or theory. When I half-believe
in reincarnation I see how little it takes
to be reborn as these citizens
who rise out of dark stone, and rage.
I broke the ground this afternoon,

heat just coming on, the shadows
without a trace of breeze.
Rooflines and junipers--this was
like the first afternoon ever,
an enduring harbor
for ease and a gardener's faith.
But their hoarded spite found me,
knew me through my clothing,
x-rayed my serenity and dismissed it.
                    The blue,
the hillside, the many sycamores
hovered mute behind their swarm.
Now try to forgive, says the harm
they needle, the ink-pain tattoo,
the slap-stun alphabet in their timeless
afterlife of scorn.

Vulture

How he lays his body
on the sky and looks
on high so graceful we want
him to be a goshawk or a falcon,
anything but what he really is.
When we stir

to final stillness, he will be
the crematorium flames,
the impersonal hunger,
separating sinew from history.
Loyal keepers of the way things really are,
over the interstate, along the frontage road,
his is the circle

over the way north.
and when we envy flight
his is what we see most often,
the wide span, the moon-tipped wings,
the gleam of the head
too small, too quick,
a pronoun with eyes.

Turtles

For long seasons we were naked hands,
quick, latticed with light,
combing the current, seizing
the scribbled verdure of the river floor.

But then the razors descended,
the winged shears that nipped
and severed, falling

into the sweeping shadows of their
own creation, lancing,
and winning, the stream
vermillion with our kind.

And so we learned.

Season by season we
took the dawn as food
made of injury and faith,

and muscled over our frailty
a new comprehension

under the rain with its herons lofting
spear-faced, the hungry day wanting us,

striding with long legs and hooked talons,
tensile, ever-famished,
never contented for long.

We drew close to our own heartbeats,
nearer to our certitude, away from

the iron annihilation
and its wings.
We willed ourselves a shield

of syllables, scored with the camouflage
of river-shadow.
And within that refuge
we were fire.

Termite Damage

The pinking shears gleam
on the blue table, the first
cold morning of the year.

All the way down to
the bay the first grass,
and last stands of
black fennel.

Throughout the long summer
the invisible teemed.
The alphabet was alive,
and secretly hungry,
consuming our home.

How hungry can they be
we ask the expert with
his white tank of poison.

I cut patterns,
calico in all
the colors of faith.

I pin the paper to the cloth,
preparing to cut habiliments
for the days to come.

How hungry, he laughs.
As hungry as everything.

Scorpion

Dry-land mesa, creosote and burrowing owls,
the subdivisions skinned
by bulldozers,
a neighborhood of carports,
swimming pools half-excavated,
backhoes parked on hummocks of sandstone.
We were happy. The interior decorator had her crystal
bowl of sliced planets and
the construction foreman had his
tattoos of vanished battleships.
Children carried books of

scarlet antidotes to the new school,
and teachers taught the crossroads
of grammar. Every autumn, when the fires ate
the hills the black ash of the alphabet
scattered over the patio slab.
Rattlesnakes coiled into fists,
escaping through the cracks
and the parsons of tardy feast,
the turkey vultures, surmounted the blue,

but these were hints compared
with the perfect embodiment of empty dark,
the ruby hook, angry at shadow,
angry at light.   Pinned under the bare heel,
midnight surprise in the bathtub,
here was the very thing,
                    the barbed
whisper come to life.

Predawn before the heat,
and late, after the sun was a memory,
the hollow walls were defiant.
Here was our home,
each temblor jiggling the bone china
in its darkness, the breathing decimal,

debt endowed with a
vengeful exoskeleton. Here
was the drought's punctuation,
the hook that separated no
from yes, the enduring
apostrophe, the fine-point
nail that willed us gone.

Sandpiper

He flies only to scurry along another
reach of surf where he
pricks the cold for prey smaller
than grains of prose. The freedom
to guess right is his autobiography, and as oracle
of the about-to-happen he prefers
the edges of day, dawn and sunset, and rainy hours

that never climb to noon.
He does not weary--his errands do not cease,
and his flight is a diary snapped open,
snapped shut, taking in no sweep
of mountain. Master of the hidden, witness

to the nameless, feasting on careers even
more unheralded than his own,
he cocks his wings
and darts with haphazard courage,
his virtuoso pause obvious to everyone
and secret.

Racoon

         He abides near
flowing water even when it's
underground, knowing how to ghost
across the cornfield to the least whisper of runoff.

He knows the truth about more than the land,
this prophet of the real.
His paws search, grasp, choose,
and his gaze glitters from a mask

of dark. Dogs fear him,
cats make a show of not seeing where he passes,
and homeowners share midnights with the hush
of his leaving.

He loses nothing,
and the wide acres are his.
He always returns, jaunty,
bold, just-this-minute gone.
And in his persistence
he learns the failings of each dwelling,

every shadow his temporary home,
the cat-door, the missing latch,
the guardian mastiff who sits back

and surrenders his meal to this
psychic of the possible,
swift but in no hurry.

The Peacock

What does he feed on,
this stalking festival,
with a gaze perpetually startled,
and a bearing so assertively free of
nest or boundary that he is either
witless or emperor of all?

Even the canary's aria
is flat beside his scarlet cry,
and he drags his multicolored
mantle like so much excess of no
use but to steady the progress
of his parade. The trailing margin
of his wealth tatters, sops mud,
scrawls the dust as he
pecks the grassy verge
of the footpath beside
the riffraff sparrow.
How many kernels of
sun and starlight he must have

snapped up in his clueless hunger,
so that in his oblivious career
he can shatter our ennui with his
ripped and ripped up
answer to the sky.

Otter

I shine like a hairless fish,
or a tongue, but this is my pelt,
enclosing a secret's cunning--
winters in dark surf have given me
the silhouette of a wave rising
or just-spent, and the cold ocean
utters me like a whisper.
                    The sand-shark
cannot catch me. The rip-fanged moray
I leave behind, and your gaze, too,
is always tardy as you call

to your companions, aim the camera,
steady the binoculars for
another look. In my
better-than-hands the stone-shelled mollusk
is a morsel, and I pluck the flashing sand-dab
from her fathoms. I'm that name
you can't remember, the language you forgot,
the hope you knew would never come,
tide departing to return.

Opossum

Fatted on the secrets of households,
he pretends to expire
right where we can see him,
round pink eyes, naked proto-hands
snout out there beyond
fur's ability to protect.

Even running
he is a being made of syncopated
clumsiness, his gait
never a lofty scamper,
but making do in unsound quickness, across
and across the street, seeming
to hurry after himself, unready
for haste. So often

road kill, time and again
the fur patch beside the creek--
this oafish wonder
ends up supplying

the ants with all
they hunger for.

Surely a first creature,
early in Creation's chapters,
and each time resembling something
escaped from a story you've never
heard before. This is the beginning,
says the small,
watery gaze. I am nothing.
But soon, soon.

The Roe Deer

for Vigdis Storsletten

The shadows of the trees
and the frost-heaved stones
over long seasons
have shaped this grazing
question, with ears
that cup the hush.

He is the thief the blossom
has desired all the untold summers,
the forager the grass
has hungered for. Awake to
the hiding place where you
believe yourself unknown,

he is the answer you
once lived, the imaginary
kingdom's real heartbeat.

Let the trees stir
above you. Draw that
deepest breath, and
keep your secret.
He knows you are here.

The Mare

In no hurry, her supple lips
take the last tassel of rye
before she turns
to eye me, long and without malice,
and she accepts my knuckles
with a solemnity
close to admonishment as I stroke
the broad, hard space between
her eyes.

And when I reach to touch her neck
she barely allows it,
her softly veined skin quick
and trembling under the advance guard
of flies. She is warm,
and silken, pulsing from within,
poised four-square
in her own shadow.
The time I do not have,
the hours I cannot spend,

are forgotten as she shakes her
mane, her ears, her entire head
with a sound like heavy
laundered clothes in a sudden breeze.
And so I search
for more, abundance

thick along the verge of the road
as she watches, her ears cocked.
And hesitates anew
as I reach through
the lengths of barbed wire
into the moist, enduring
query of her breath.

The Moth

There is one now,
on the screen door,
his chalky wings a blur,
wanting in, wanting in.
A neighbor arrives,
headlights and the thump of a car door.
The voices slip
through the geometry of lights
thrown down by the front windows and a few words
break through more clearly than others,
as we smell the hint of a cigarette.

The warm weather begins at dawn,
and lasts long after sundown.
We fought against it,
sitting beside the air-conditioner all day,
but now we have this quiet vigil,
nothing more to be done.

Everything is open,
the windows, the front door
with its screened darkness.
When a dog passes
we hear the tinkle of its collar tags.

Above the old orange tree in the garden
the silhouette of the mountain rises up and then the stars
and the satellites take over. The tiny points that move
look exactly like the ones that don't,
silence followed by silence.

The moth climbs, flies in place,
and climbs yet more.
We sit quiet and the house around us
is still, and of all the living things he
is the most urgent, endlessly on his way
with the earth toward morning.

Magpie Harm

They blind the lambs
these black and white birds,
traveling in pairs across the rain-dark lawn.
They're dangerous and despicable,
argues my friend, recognizing
their cruelty year by year

as long as flocks have bred.
It is a cold day, a city
brittle with traffic.
Where is there a way
vehicle fumes and coal sweat
have not soiled?

Two of the birds are searching
the grass beyond the stretching
chestnut tree roots, twin
assassins in the late afternoon.
And I get ready to tell my companion that

these birds take no joy in destruction,
nor in the agony of the new-born.
They gather new-minted pennies and
dazzling buttons, isn't that the legend?

Planning nests of treasures,
they wing across the iron land
each evening, disappointed
in the taste of blood.

Mosquito

The garden at night is coy shadow,
fishpond thick with softly
gleaming algae.
The human whispers, our murmured
secret, thrives in such balmy
chiaroscuro and we have so
much to share--but we
are not alone. The insistent,
stubborn needles, yes,
no, approach and flee, their
whine more distracting than any song.
The wounds they leave are nagging
constellations across the map
we wear within our clothes,

as the hunters easily know here we have
hidden in the windless angle of the dark.
The hand slaps, misses, kills, what does

it matter? They are legion,
and what they steal is hungrily
pilfered survival.
We slap again,

shake our heads, wave our hands, too much,
soon we will escape.
But stay, almost forgiving--we have
so much to learn about
each other and these hungry

wings pause only to persist,
missing, stealing with a
blue-note *mine, mine.*

The Louse

        Gray semi-colon,
many-legged full-stop,
battener on the slightest taste
of existence, you sift from mortal
to mortal by way of our assignations,
our beds your season of migration.
And while some memento of affection
would not be regretted,

what troubles your human host
at last is not the individual
refugee who lingers,
or the sole conqueror who survives
on carnal damp. No,
the crisis arises through teeming,
the ellipses multiplied into a horde,
until one evening in the candlelight

even the stripped denims harbor
the torpid, dazzled throngs

of ash-pale afterthought,
blind nature's solution

to nothing in particular, as though
Tourette's Syndrome broke a new
barrier, a speaker who bursts out
not in profanity but in lint,
erasure crumbs, dust motes,
the once-covert chaff now
flavored with our lives.

Lizard Hunt

        The light is her
body, she is made of it,
and she has a heartbeat while before
she had only one-plus-one.
She multiplies, breath times sight times
the taste of the air. She was wrong,
but now she's right. She knows.
She sees your slow, primordial grasp,

your boyhood ache for aimless trophies
as a threat like the coyote's
or the roadrunner's but far, far
less competent, and she sees your slowly

focusing gaze and
takes in all you are,
moment by even slower moment,
you, reaching and in a spasm of quickness
seizing.
        Even when

she leaves her tail to dance, even when she
leaves what looked like half her living body,
half her life on earth.

Jack Rabbit

With his claw-hammer ears,
and his too-big hind legs
he's too fleet to be
graceful, in flight
all air, away and away, erratic

and determined.
We want so much.
All summer we schemed,
where to store hopes,
how to spend them.
The fire crews along the two-lane
burned the brush,
creosote and sage,
searing it all to black,

and still the long season
would never end.
It ends now.

Even to see
where I escape
he says, you will

be forced and forced
again to ignorance.
Fire char, struck

by his leap, smoking
carbon. Now and now,
slashed mesquite,

flung rye-weed, liberator
from boredom, thief
of expectation. Gone.
And still there.

Hibernation

The sky has vanished and
the bear cannot be seen.

Day has gone, and night is all there is,
from the beginning to this present

instant with its wrinkled glacier.
The bear sleeps in the earth,

and the land is blank, white
starlight over empty ice.

The bear stirs but does not wake.
Moss and lichen

are buried under ceaseless
silence, slope and ridge

turned to glass.

Even the wind is ancient,
weighing down on every

uncovered stone,
suppressing every hue.

This is midnight as the bear

slumbers underground.
This is predawn, nothing changed. This is

his increasingly broken dream,
his flagging sleep, progressively imperfect

oblivion, breaking light
through the chapters of soil.

This is hunger rising in the east.

The Giraffe

Let the trees
root and grow.
Let the feeding birds choose this
shade or that branch.
When the learned accept
that the lessons are worn out,
only the wide horizon is left,
and a life shaped by such

magnitude is changed,
elevated in a way
that can only be awkward.
To be handsome, he realizes,
accepting this
clumsy grandeur, to be a
creature of proportion,
is hopeless. And so he feeds
from the crests of the woodland,
follows a shadow ungainly but fluid,

over the watering hole,
through the increasingly scattered salt lick,
over the tracks of lesser, quicker beings,
their diminutive elegance exhausted
by escape from the predators
that only the extraordinary can see,
and only the silent ungainly,
resigned to his stature, free of hope,
can drive from the helpless.

Elephant At the Mall Grand Opening

The snout is delicate, snuffling, pursuing the peanut and
extending further. Considering.
Two gouts of hot exhalation,
saluting, curling around the twin-nuggets
of the peanut shell and bringing the small woody legume to
      a mouth
like a secret smile and then the exchange is done.

No more, nothing else to give.
But nonetheless the prehensile
poke-holes breathe, trespass on my shirt front and
      shoulder,
and gently, shockingly softly, cross my face.
The elm-tree wrinkles around his eyes are equalled by
seams throughout his girth.
The eyes are so small, the feet so flat and ponderously right
exactly there,

and shifting unalterably in the following new position,
so weightily emphatic that

the manure just dropped on the sidewalk
is instantly trodden to flat, golden soil.
Even his shadow takes a long heart-beat
to shift and flow, passing with his keeper's

metal prod as the weather passes, climate
altering as the world settles on.
And yet he turns back, half a planet taking a long moment
in apparent curiosity at a stranger's bounty, wondering if
another gift might be in the offing,

so fully present, so immediately searching
with his ears shrugging upward like awnings and his skin
flowing with the argument of
muscles over his bones, that nothing can happen, now,
nothing but this great animal's wonder.

The Flea

For him the truth is a flavor,
a pulse made of nutriment,
a living mountain of breath.
Even pinched between
the fingers and released, he springs
to perfect absence, beyond punishment,
a celebrant of undetectable freedom.
Cinder-speck, a vibrant

fiend of punctuation,
no bigger than a typesetter's
semicolon, there he is again.
And again. He leaves tiny misery,
his wound angry but subtle,
a meal cadged by a parasite whose disguise
is the squirrel's scurry,
or the mastiff's drowse.
Hiding when he cannot leap, he is a fugitive

who stays where he is, misery to the tomcat,
vexation to the hound,

purveyor of infection in hosts
too mute upon the summer field

to know the name of what
steals their peace.
Now he says, meaning then.
Here he says, meaning there. Too late.

The Flamingo

The pink of her plumage
is borrowed from the shells of shrimp she
snaps from the muddy grasses, as step-by-step
she extends her stride across
a kingdom not river, not sea,

safe because she is a replica
of another and another, copies every one.
She gazes. She gazes again,
                    a hunter
of no cunning, a swimmer of no depth.
Even her beauty is doubtful--
peering, straightening,
she drips water from a beak
too bent to be a weapon, too mute for song.
Emptily alert, she is

as tall as she needs to be
to attend to the multitude
that feeds in salt-shallows trodden green,
rises to cloud the sun,

and descends again to
reedy afterthought. Nothing is hers.

Eagle

for Sara Van den Bossche

She releases the earth,
every dawn, opens
like day and closes like night.
The human highway
is nothing to her,
blunt in its purpose,

coursing to no destination
she calls home. The squirrel's
chatter, the flycatcher's shrill
empty gossip beneath her shadow,
no rumor scores her quiet.
All night
she wakes, and wakes again,
nothing to tell, no story

to sound, the broken syllables of the lake,
the susurration of the river her
names for hunger.

Her talons seize the steelhead
and grasp the trout,
but in a kingdom of pinprick
birdsong she is the tidings,
now and now, echoing nothing,
prey to no rumor, silence her anthem.

The Crocodile

This ruse, enduring for days,
will eventually cease, but now
even the birds mistake him for a log,
or a stone the fleeting drought
has lifted above the current.
Because there is a current, even in this cocoa-dark

side-pool, and the solution to hiding
so plainly under the sun is to glide as
the magnolia petals do, or the fallen limb of a tree,
as though alive not at all—except secretly,
to hunger.

                     No other creature
could survive and be so torpid.
And yet he is ready,
the humid vault of the wetland
his camouflage. Wit and song
he leaves for others, prime

in his vigil, knowing without
memory, trusting without faith.
The door of his heartbeat opens,

and the same door slowly shuts. His sleep
and his waking are the same. Noon

sifts downward, and then the sunset
and soon, he knows, surely
very soon some quicker more beautiful
sojourner will discover
with what swiftness comes the end.

Cat

She arrives again
when you've given up,
let the past go,
begun a future of no certain
value, put away last
night's dishes,
and said to yourself almost

believing it that continuing
is a kind of faith, a small
acceptance of every night.
And as you sit and cross off
the list, things to do, requirements

for the days ahead, she steals
past you, letting her
silence slide along
the hem of your solitude.
And settles just,
just beyond your reach.

Bee Swarm

Diving into its own intensity,
getting all the time greater
in noise and force. A frantic, powerful
entity not connected with the dawn or the night,
an inflamed person risen up furiously
primed, and not nearly finished, getting
greater in girth and sound

with a timbre like a Gregorian single-note, a swell of voices
enthralled by its own harmonics.
A slowly lifting gordian knot
of riot that sparks
flint-chips, amber arrow-points, a fighting host
hovering and casting a boiling shadow
above the sidewalk where the frail ivy
has just the day before been
tucked into the erosion-wrinkled land,

the wan green flags of the novice ground-cover nothing,
not even living, compared with this

muscled rage that by an hour's
tumult is absent, gone, two or three
spent winged splinters of the once-great
concord left behind on the ground,
while everything else has swept onward
to the places where day hides its power.

The Bee

A ricochet,
she races, lingers,
hurries to be forgotten,
the single vowel of a teeming alphabet,
too small to carry meaning.
Privation and bright colors,

these are what stir the amber full-stop,
this fragment made of hunger.
Dawn too cool,
noon too hot, where is peace
for this searcher? The chapter is the same,
beginning and beginning,

another blossom with a secret nearly as sweet
as its promise.
Almost followed by almost,

she survives beyond knowledge.
Even her dance of distance and direction
is the gavotte of decimals learning a new

place among the zeroes, notes finding a new
high-point within the octave as she

zig-zags, color to color,
clover to fuchsia to sage
in the only daylight.

Ants

This is the earth before
anyone laughed.
This is the persistent prehistoric
republic rising up along the wall,
escaping the rising groundwater trying
not to drown.

And in drought,
theirs are the hunters,
far from safety, groping
toward the still-moist sponge.

I marvel at their stubborn
multitude around
the stillborn robin's chick but
I will not applaud them.
Here they are,

their long queue busy
all the way to the stored
Christmas candy under the bed.

Here is a solitary soldier
looking too small to have a pulse.
He feels his way, he feels his way across
the lighted sink top, so sure and even more sure--
he is so continual with his searching,
molecule-tipped limbs that

I lift my hand
and can't. I can't let the brute
palm fall as the illumination of the kitchen
and the daylight progress under
his intricate shadow and he stays in
one place, groping
as beneath him crawls the world.

Michael Cadnum is the author of thirty-seven books, including the National Book Award finalist *The Book of the Lion* (Viking) and *Peril on the Sea* (Farrar, Straus & Giroux.) He lives in Albany, California, with his wife Sherina.

Author photo © 2018 Sherina Cadnum

Made in the USA
San Bernardino, CA
02 March 2020